TATE BRITAIN
HIGHLIGHTS

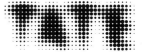

FOREWORD
ALEX FARQUHARSON
DIRECTOR, TATE BRITAIN

Welcome to Tate Britain, home to the national collection of British art from the Tudor period to the present day. This guide has been designed to offer visitors a brief overview and introduction to the collection's highlights and to demonstrate something of its remarkable range. Only a small selection of the works on display could be included in these pages, but each has been chosen to describe something of the overall collection and to provide an impression of a walk through the gallery. Similarly the works of art included here are arranged in chronological order, mirroring the way we have displayed the collection since 2013, beginning with the north-west galleries, which are the most ornate and classical, and ending in the north-east part of the building, where we find ourselves within modern 'white cube' spaces built in the late 1970s.

Interspersed between the individual artworks in this book are seven special features – focusing more closely on the work of William Blake, J.M.W. Turner, the Pre-Raphaelites, Henry Moore, Barbara Hepworth, Francis Bacon and David Hockney. These celebrated names have been selected because they are all particularly well represented in Tate's collection and we are fortunate to own many of their best-known works on behalf of the nation. No artist, arguably, is more important to Tate Britain than Turner. The unique Turner Bequest is owned by Tate and housed in the Clore Gallery, a space dedicated to the artist. The bequest is staggering in size and includes all the works that Turner had in his possession at the time of his death in 1851, which amounts to several hundred oil paintings and sketchbooks and thousands of watercolours. Blake and Moore also have rooms dedicated solely to their work at Tate Britain, while in St Ives, Cornwall, Tate operates a museum devoted to Hepworth in her former studio and garden.

The story of British art at Tate

Tate Britain, with its focus on British art from the 16th century to today, is unique within the Tate family of galleries, which is otherwise devoted to international modern and contemporary art. Indeed, no other museum in the world has quite the same remit. The national parameters at Tate Britain allow visitors to experience the long story of art from the Renaissance right up to the present day, not only in its collection but also in our exhibition programme (Tate Britain is, for example, the home of the renowned contemporary art award, the Turner Prize).

British art is remarkable for the dominance of portraiture, at least to 1800, and landscape, especially during the Romantic age (roughly 1790–1830). Sculpture becomes more prevalent in the modern era, from the 1910s to the1960s – represented here by the likes of Jacob Epstein and Anthony Caro – and surfaces again in the 1980s, in the hands of Antony Gormley among others.

British art is also notable for genres unique to itself: group portraits, known as 'conversation pieces', focusing on social relations between friends, family and allies; themes from British literature, particularly Shakespeare, Milton and Tennyson (rather than classical mythology);

In 2017, Rachel Whiteread's *Untitled (One Hundred Spaces)* 1995 was installed in Tate Britain's Duveen galleries during her exhibition.

and topical subjects in the late 18th and early 19th centuries reflecting the wars with France and the scientific innovations of the Industrial Revolution. Hogarth ushered in an art of social engagement, as did the artists associated with the Young British Art movement more recently. By contrast, Blake, a little-known figure in his day, has inspired two or three waves of dream-like, esoteric British art in the 19th and 20th centuries (and countless poets and musicians).

Despite the apparent 'Britishness' of these traits in British art, our remit at Tate Britain is better described as art made in Britain than British art. From the outset, British painting was as much the creation of artist-exiles as it was home-grown talent. Among the artists appearing in these pages Gheeraerts, Siberechts and van Dyck were Flemish, Lely was Dutch, Kauffman and Fuseli were Swiss, Copley, Whistler and Sargent were American as was Epstein, Sickert and Freud were German by birth as is Tillmans, Gabo was Russian, Souza was Indian, and Bowling and Himid were born in Guyana and Tanzania respectively. British art, for centuries, has been shaped by the contributions of artist-émigrés. And, as often as not, the art history – and history – that the collection narrates is as much about the world as it is about Britain.

Art has a rich and complex relationship to its social and cultural contexts. Sometimes that relationship is directly expressed; often it is subtly implicit or indirectly conveyed. The art from Britain in Tate's collection is rich with imaginative invention and reinvention, and our exhibitions and displays aim to celebrate this aesthetic ingenuity as an ongoing story. At the same time, a walk through Tate Britain reveals how 500 years of art can act as a fascinating lens through which to deepen our understanding of ourselves and society, past and present, in both Britain and in the rest of world.

I very much hope you enjoy your visit and thank you for buying this book – every purchase goes towards supporting Tate, its work and upkeep of the collection.

Martin Boyce's *Remembered Skies* 2017 was specially commissioned by Tate Britain with the support of the Clore Duffield Foundation. It is situated outside the Clore Gallery – the home of the Turner Bequest.

TATE BRITAIN
A BRIEF HISTORY

The Tate galleries are named after Henry Tate, a Victorian businessman who made his fortune through refining sugar and manufacturing sugar cubes. He was also one of Britain's most important art collectors.

In 1889 he offered to donate his collection to the nation on the condition that a suitable gallery was built to display it. The National Gallery of British Art opened to the public in 1897. It was designed by architect Sydney Smith, and built on the former site of Millbank Penitentiary, once the largest prison in Europe and a departure point for sending convicts to Australia.

Originally founded as a branch of the National Gallery, in 1917 the gallery was made responsible for forming a national collection of modern international art as well as British art. It was officially renamed as the Tate Gallery in 1932 and finally became completely independent of the National Gallery in 1954.

Today there are four Tate Galleries across the country. Tate Liverpool opened in 1988, Tate St Ives in 1993 and

John Lavery, *The Opening of the Modern Foreign and Sargent Galleries at the Tate Gallery, 26 June 1926* exhibited 1929

Tate Modern in 2000. Tate Modern opened on the site of the former Bankside Power Station in London and shows international modern and contemporary art. With the opening of Tate Modern, the Tate Gallery was renamed Tate Britain and returned to its original role as a centre for British art.

Patrons and the gallery building

Henry Tate gave 65 pictures to the new gallery, including John Everett Millais's *Ophelia* and J.W. Waterhouse's *The Lady of Shalott*, but perhaps his most important gift was the money he gave to build the gallery. Since then many artists and patrons have influenced the collection and the building. J.M.W. Turner, for example, left 300 oil paintings and over 30,000 works on paper to the nation in his will. In 1910, 60 years after his death, the Tate expanded the galleries dedicated to his gift, and 70 years later opened another in the form of the Clore Gallery, designed by architect James Stirling and supported by the Clore Foundation.

Other significant patrons include the Duveen family, who funded large extensions to the gallery, including the Turner Galleries in 1910, the Modern Foreign and Sargent Galleries in 1926, and, in 1937, the two 90-metre-long Sculpture Galleries that run down the middle of the building. In 2000, new exhibition galleries and a new entrance to the side of the gallery were designed by John Miller and Partners, and named after the benefactors, the Linbury Trust and Edwin Manton. The most recent additions to the building (by architects Caruso St John and completed in 2013) are a large spiral staircase to the lower level, a new café, schools' areas and members' rooms.

Floods and war damage

In January 1928 the River Thames breached its banks after heavy rains and flooded the gallery with muddy water. The prompt action of Tate staff and volunteers ensured that most of the artworks were safely salvaged. Just two months earlier, the artist Rex Whistler had finished a series of murals to decorate the walls of the restaurant. Amazingly they were unharmed, despite being submerged in 2.5 metres of flood water. Sadly, a number of artworks which were stored in the basement were badly damaged. Today, the Tate Store in Southwark provides a state-of-the-art storage facility for works which are not on display.

The Tate Gallery was a vulnerable target during the Second World War. The gallery was closed to the public in 1939; large sculptures and paintings were placed in blast-proof storage in the basement of the building, and the rest of the art was evacuated. Green Park Underground Station and (from 1941) disused tunnels at Piccadilly Station were used for storage, and the bulk of the collection was dispersed to three private country houses.

In September 1940 the Tate Gallery was hit by a high explosive bomb. The director, John Rothenstein, had moved into the gallery, and was woken 'by a terrific explosion to feel the massive building violently shaking and to hear an avalanche of masonry and glass'. This was just the first of an almost nightly barrage of bombs that rained on the building and its grounds. In 1942 the gallery garden was converted into allotments for local residents, and in 1944 pre-fabricated homes were sited in the grounds behind the building to provide temporary accommodation for people made homeless by the bombing raids. Shrapnel damage to the gallery caused by bombs can still be seen on the outside walls, particularly at the Manton entrance on Atterbury Street.

Tate Archive
Also housed at Tate Britain is the Tate Archive. This is the national archive for British art since 1900, with more than twenty million pieces and over 900 collections. It includes letters, writings, preparatory artworks, sketchbooks, audio-visual material, photographs, posters and press cuttings.

Carrying pictures to safety during the flood of 1928

Artworks returning from wartime storage in the London Underground (the central work is *Wake* by Edward Burra)

John Bettes
A Man in a Black Cap 1545

This is the earliest picture in the Tate collection. The artist's name is marked on the back, and the inscriptions on the front indicate that the work was painted 'in the year of our Lord 1545' and that the sitter was 26 years old. Bettes is first recorded as carrying out decorative work for Henry VIII's court in 1531–3, and he may have worked with Hans Holbein the Younger, the most famous Tudor painter. Originally this portrait was larger and would have had a blue background similar to the colour often used by Holbein. Long exposure to light, however, has changed the pigment (smalt) to brown.

Marcus Gheeraerts II
Portrait of Captain Thomas Lee 1594

Marcus Gheeraerts II was a Netherlandish artist who worked at the court of Queen Elizabeth I. This portrait of Thomas Lee, who served in the English colonial forces in Ireland, is highly political and full of symbolism. Lee was suspected of treachery to the queen, but here he declares his loyalty. While his expensive lace, exquisite embroidery and finely inlaid pistol express his gentlemanly status, his bare legs echo not only the dress of a poor Irish foot soldier but also a Roman hero. The Latin inscription in the tree refers to the Roman Mucius Scaevola, who stayed true to Rome even when among its enemies, and its inclusion implies that Lee too is faithful.

Unknown Artist
The Cholmondeley Ladies c.1600–10

According to the inscription at the bottom left, this painting shows 'Two Ladies of the Cholmondeley Family, Who were born the same day, Married the same day, And brought to Bed [gave birth] the same day'. Though the painting is traditionally said to depict sisters, small details such as the colour of their eyes show they are not identical twins.

David Des Granges
The Saltonstall Family c.1636–7

This grand painting is thought to show Sir Richard Saltonstall and his family. The pallid figure in the bed may be a posthumous image of Sir Richard's first wife, gesturing towards the couple's two surviving children. Sir Richard gazes towards his second – living – wife, who sits holding her own Saltonstall baby. The artist's inspiration here appears to have been the elaborate family tombs of the period.

Anthony van Dyck
Portrait of Sir William Killigrew 1638

The Flemish artist van Dyck was the most significant portrait painter in England at the time. Internationally famous, the relaxed ease and grace he bestowed on his sitters transformed British portraiture. He worked for the court of Charles I and portrayed many of the leading figures at a time of political turmoil that led to the English Civil War. Sir William Killigrew (1606–95) was a courtier to Charles I and later also a playwright. He is shown leaning meditatively against the base of a column. A ring, tied by a ribbon to his black satin jacket, may allude romantically to his wife or denote mourning for a friend or relative.

Peter Lely
Two Ladies of the Lake Family c.1660

The Dutch painter Lely was working in England from the 1640s but, following the Restoration of 1660 and Charles II's return from exile, he became the King's Principal Painter. Through this office he achieved significant prominence and his large, busy and highly influential portrait studio was a dominant force until his death in 1680. The precise identities of the women here are not known for certain, and the artist is more concerned with depicting a sense of glamour and sophistication than conveying individual personalities. The woman on the left is shown playing a French-made guitar, the latest fashion to arrive from Paris.

Mary Beale
Portrait of a Young Girl c.1681

Mary Beale was the most prolific professional female portrait painter working in England in the 17th century. This engagingly informal oil sketch was one of a number of experiments with different painting techniques that she produced at this time. Her aim was to improve the speed and efficiency of her studio's portrait production, for example finishing a work in one session rather than the more costly and time-consuming four or five. We know that Beale used members of her family and studio as models for such works; the girl here is probably her god-daughter or her female studio assistant.

Jan Siberechts
View of a House and its Estate in Belsize, Middlesex 1696

When this painting was made, the area of Belsize belonged to the Dean and Chapter of Westminster Abbey (the abbey itself can be seen on the horizon). Today, Belsize Park is part of north-west London, but in 1696 it was a distant country retreat for affluent middle-class Londoners. The central building may be the house of John Coggs, a London goldsmith and banker. The painting was probably commissioned by him to act as a portrait of his property. The Antwerp-born painter Jan Siberechts arrived in London in the 1670s and became one of England's leading landscape painters, specialising in such bird's-eye views of country estates.

William Hogarth
O the Roast Beef of Old England
('The Gate of Calais') 1748

Hogarth achieved enormous success
with his satirical images of modern life,
which were designed to be 'read' like
the emerging literary form of the novel.
He visited France in 1748 and while
sketching the fortifications at Calais was
suspected of spying and arrested (shown
at the left of the painting: an officer's hand
clasps his shoulder). Hogarth represents
the French as a rabble of scrawny soldiers
and a fat friar, salivating over a haunch
of beef imported for the British. Hogarth
contrasts France implicitly with an England
where everyone eats roast beef and not
soupe maigre (watery soup).

Joshua Reynolds
Colonel Acland and Lord Sydney:
The Archers 1769

Reynolds painted this life-size portrait shortly after he became the first president of the Royal Academy of Arts. The scale and style of the work demonstrate his desire to elevate portraiture to the level of 'high art' alongside the genre of history painting, which was traditionally seen as superior. The depiction of the two sitters dressed in medieval-style clothing and hunting with bows and arrows reflects a fashion for archery in aristocratic circles at this time, with its virile and romantic associations. The subjects are shown in perfect harmony – at one with each other and joint masters over nature.

Angelica Kauffman
Portrait of a Lady c.1775

The unknown woman in this portrait is dressed in classical robes and seated by a statue of Minerva, the goddess of wisdom. The depiction of a female sitter with the tools of learning – the book on the table and the writing materials in her hand – points to the developments in women's education in the second half of the 18th century. Born in Switzerland, Kauffman lived in England between 1766 and 1781. In recognition of her professional standing, she was one of only two female founder members of the Royal Academy in 1768.

Joseph Wright of Derby
Sir Brooke Boothby 1781

Brooke Boothby was a Derbyshire landowner and an amateur poet and philosopher. Wright shows him reclining by a stream, holding a book with 'Rousseau' on its spine. This is a reference to Boothby's pride in having published the first volume of the Swiss-born philosopher's autobiographical *Dialogues* in 1780. By depicting the poet lying down in a woodland setting, Wright has attempted to convey Rousseau's belief in the importance of man living in harmony with nature.

Thomas Gainsborough
Giovanna Baccelli exhibited 1782

Gainsborough was the foremost British portrait painter of the second half of the 18th century. This portrait shows the famous Italian dancer Giovanna Zanerini, known on the stage as Baccelli, at the height of her career. Her elaborate costume seems to be adapted from the ballet *Les Amants surpris*, in which she had recently taken London by storm. The rapid brushwork, translucent paint and shimmering light effects are typical of Gainsborough's style at this time. When the portrait was first exhibited it was chiefly praised as an excellent likeness: 'as the Original, light airy and elegant'.

John Singleton Copley
The Death of Major Peirson,
6 January 1781 1783

This picture celebrates the British defence
of Jersey against French invasion in 1781
and also pays tribute to a young major,
Francis Peirson, who lost his life in the
process. The Anglo-American Copley
increased the drama of the scene by
making the moment of Peirson's death
coincide with the final British victory over
the French, when in fact he was killed
shortly before the battle. The theme of
the modern noble hero expiring at the
scene of battle was popular at this time,
and the painting drew crowds when it
was first exhibited.

WILLIAM BLAKE

William Blake developed radical new approaches to painting and printmaking to explore highly personal interpretations of Christian themes. While esteemed today, during his lifetime Blake was appreciated by only a handful of artists and collectors, and generally regarded as an oddball visionary.

Songs of Innocence and Experience: Infant Sorrow 1794, reprinted 1831 or later (above)

Songs of Innocence and Experience is a double set of illustrated poems showing 'the Two Contrary States of the Human Soul': the childlike and pure versus the angry and disillusioned. This poem is a contrast to 'Infant Joy'. Blake combined poetry and art, with the words, figures and ornament all drawn directly on to copperplate by the artist.

The Ghost of a Flea c.1819–20 (left)

Blake claimed to have seen visions daily since his boyhood. Later, with his friend the astrologer John Varley, he would try to summon spirits and then sketch them. This creature appeared to Blake in a vision, telling him that all fleas were inhabited by the souls of men, who were 'by nature bloodthirsty to excess'.

Newton 1795–c.1805 (left)

Blake portrays Isaac Newton crouched naked on a rock covered with algae, apparently at the bottom of the sea. His attention is focused on a diagram which he draws with a compass. Blake was critical of Newton's reductive, scientific approach and so shows him merely following the rules of his compass, blind to the colourful rocks behind him.

Satan Smiting Job with Sore Boils c.1826 (below)

In the biblical Book of Job, God and Satan discuss the limits of human faith and endurance. God lets Satan force Job to undergo extreme trials and tribulations, including the destruction of his family. Despite this, as God predicted, Job's faith remains unshaken and he is rewarded by God with the restoration of his health, wealth and family. Here Blake shows Satan torturing Job by afflicting his body with boils.

Henry Fuseli
Titania and Bottom c.1790

Swiss-born Fuseli is known for his
paintings of the supernatural.
This work, commissioned by the
publisher John Boydell as part of his
'Shakespeare Gallery', illustrates a
scene from *A Midsummer Night's Dream*
in which the fairy queen Titania is
punished for her pride by her husband,
Oberon. He casts a spell that makes
her fall in love with Bottom, whose
head has been magically replaced
with that of an ass. Fuseli was Professor
of Painting at the Royal Academy and
his style had a considerable influence
on many younger British artists,
including William Blake.

Thomas Lawrence
Mrs Siddons 1804

Lawrence was the most popular
English portrait painter of his time,
famed for portraying most of the
high-society personalities of the day
in his polished and flattering style.
His international reputation was
secured when the Prince Regent
(later King George IV) commissioned
Lawrence to paint portraits of all the
foreign leaders involved in the defeat
of Napoleon. He painted many portraits
of Sarah Siddons, known as the greatest
tragic actress of her age. She is shown
at one of her dramatic readings,
with volumes of plays beside her.

J.M.W. TURNER

Tate Britain is home to the largest collection of works by Joseph Mallord William Turner. A master of history, landscape and marine painting, he challenged the style of the Old Masters, trailblazing in technique and subject matter. Described as the 'father of modern art', Turner often shocked his contemporaries with his loose brushwork and vibrant colour palette while portraying the development of the modern world unlike any other artist at the time.

The Battle of Trafalgar, as Seen from the Mizen Starboard Shrouds of the 'Victory' 1806–8 (below)

In this painting of the battle in which Admiral Nelson died, Turner makes close observation of the ships, but the painting is not simply detailed reportage. Sails and cannon smoke fill the picture, creating a claustrophobic backdrop, while the action appears to thrust outwards. The viewer is confronted by both the chaos of battle and the intimate tragedy of Nelson's final moments. A reviewer at the time described it as a 'British epic picture ... the first picture of the kind that has ever been exhibited'.

Rome, from the Vatican. Raffaelle, Accompanied by La Fornarina, Preparing his Pictures for the Decoration of the Loggia exhibited 1820 (above)

Turner was at the height of his fame when he first visited Rome. This painting, exhibited shortly after he returned to London in 1820, distils the rich variety of experiences he had enjoyed. The picture was created to mark the 300th anniversary of the great Italian Renaissance artist Raphael's death.

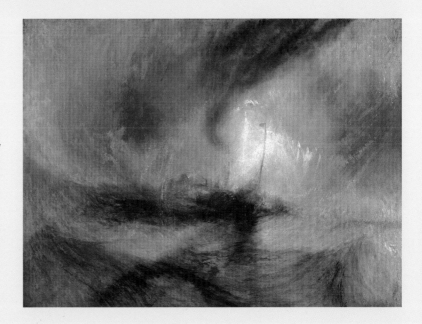

Snow Storm – Steam-Boat off a Harbour's Mouth exhibited 1842 (right)

Turner painted many pictures exploring the effects of an elemental vortex. Here there is a steamboat at the heart of the vortex. It is famously said that Turner created this image while lashed to the mast of a ship during an actual storm at sea. This seems to be nothing more than fiction, but the story has endured as a way of demonstrating Turner's full-blooded engagement with the world around him.

John Simpson
Head of a Man (?Ira Frederick Aldridge)
exhibited 1827

This portrait is probably of the actor
Ira Frederick Aldridge. He also appears
in a related work by Simpson, *The
Captive Slave*, exhibited in 1827. It is
not clear whether Aldridge was working
as a model, or whether these portraits
were created to showcase how versatile
he was as an actor. Although the slave
trade had been made illegal in 1807,
slavery continued in British colonies
until the 1830s and remained a divisive
political issue.

John Constable
Salisbury Cathedral from the Meadows
exhibited 1831

Constable started painting large-scale
landscapes to attract more notice at the
Royal Academy exhibitions and to project
his ideas about landscape. This is the
most spectacular of his monumental
paintings. When it was first exhibited it
didn't sell, and it remained in his studio
– where he continued to retouch it – until
his death in 1837. Constable believed that
one day it would be seen as his finest
picture, saying 'I have no doubt of this
picture being my best now'. The rainbow
only appeared in this final iteration.

PRE-RAPHAELITES

In 1848 a group of rebellious young artists, frustrated
by the work of the older generation of painters, founded
the Pre-Raphaelite Brotherhood. Led by William Holman
Hunt, Dante Gabriel Rossetti and John Everett Millais,
the group rejected the loose brushwork and heavy, dark
tones of contemporary painting. Instead, they painted
with small brushes and bright colours in imitation
of what they considered the purer vision of artists
working before the Renaissance painter Raphael.

John Everett Millais
Ophelia 1851–2 (left)

This work depicts the death of Ophelia from Shakespeare's *Hamlet*. Driven mad with grief when Hamlet murders her father, Polonius, she falls into a stream and drowns. The flowers she holds are symbolic: the poppy signifies death, daisies innocence and pansies love in vain. The painting was regarded in its day as one of the most accurate and elaborate studies of nature ever made. The background was painted from life by the Hogsmill River in Surrey. The artists' model Elizabeth Siddall posed for *Ophelia* in a bath of water kept warm by lamps positioned underneath.

William Holman Hunt
The Awakening Conscience 1853 (right)

This painting shows a wealthy man visiting his mistress in an apartment which he has provided for her. The tune which he idly plays on the piano has reminded her of her past, and she rises from his lap towards the bright outside world (made visible to the viewer in the mirror). The claustrophobic space is filled with intricate clues, such as the bird trying to escape from a cat and the female figure enclosed in a glass dome, which echoes the shape of the painting.

Henry Wallis
Chatterton 1856 (above)

This highly romanticised picture created a sensation when it was first exhibited at the Royal Academy in 1856. Thomas Chatterton was a poet whose Gothic writings, melancholic life and suicide at the age of 17 fascinated artists and writers of the 19th century. At an early age Chatterton wrote fake medieval histories and poems, which he copied onto old parchment and passed off as manuscripts from the Middle Ages. In London he struggled to earn a living, writing tales and songs for popular publications. Penniless, he took his own life in 1770 by swallowing arsenic.

Dante Gabriel Rossetti
Beata Beatrix c.1864–70 (right)

The inspiration for this work was the medieval Italian poet Dante's 'Vita Nuova', which explores his idealised love for Beatrice and his grief at her premature death. As an omen of death, a bird drops a white poppy between her open hands. In the background the ghostly Dante gazes towards the figure of Love. Rossetti viewed this work as a memorial to his wife, Elizabeth Siddall – the model for Beatrice – who had died in 1862.

Edward Coley Burne-Jones
The Golden Stairs 1880 (right)

The artist simply described his subject here as 'a procession of girls coming down a flight of stairs'. With its elaborate surface patterns and lack of clear narrative, the painting might be purely decorative, conveying the idea of endless movement. One underlying theory popular at the time was that 'all art constantly aspires towards the condition of music'.

Richard Dadd
The Fairy Feller's Master-Stroke 1855–64

Richard Dadd painted this work in the Bethlem psychiatric hospital (now the Imperial War Museum), where he was sent after murdering his father and being declared insane. Oberon and Titania, from Shakespeare's *A Midsummer Night's Dream*, appear in the top half of the picture, but the rest of the figures are drawn from the artist's imagination. The main focus is the 'Fairy Feller', poised to split a large chestnut which will be used to construct Queen Mab's new fairy carriage. Dadd worked on the painting for nine years, paying microscopic attention to detail, layering paint to produce almost three-dimensional results.

Frederic Leighton
An Athlete Wrestling with a Python 1877

This work is said to have started a revival in British sculpture, which had become neglected by artists. Leighton's fresh approach looked back to classical sculpture but focused on a more natural and detailed representation of the human body. This coincided with a revival of interest in sculpting in bronze. This work was made using the lost-wax technique, allowing for precision in composition.

James Abbott McNeill Whistler
Nocturne: Blue and Silver – Chelsea 1871

Whistler sketched this view from Battersea Bridge looking across the Thames towards Chelsea. A fisherman stands in the foreground looking out to a low barge. It was the first of Whistler's series of *Nocturnes*: paintings intended to convey a sense of the beauty and tranquillity of the river in the evening or by night. Making a parallel between painting and music, Whistler titled many of his paintings 'Arrangements', 'Harmonies' or 'Nocturnes'. 'A nocturne', he said, 'is an arrangement of line, form and colour.'

John Singer Sargent
Carnation, Lily, Lily, Rose 1885–6

Sargent was considered the leading portrait painter of his generation and was commissioned by many of the distinguished personalities of his day. For this picture the models were daughters of a friend. Wanting to capture the exact level of light at dusk, he painted the picture outdoors, using impressionist painting techniques he had learned in Paris from his friend Claude Monet. He painted every day from September to November 1885 in the few minutes when he felt the light was perfect. The title comes from the chorus of a song popular at the time.

John William Waterhouse
The Lady of Shalott 1888

This painting shows the tragic scene which concludes Alfred, Lord Tennyson's poem 'The Lady of Shalott' (1842). The heroine is forbidden by a curse to look directly at the world, instead being doomed to view reality through a mirror. After the knight Sir Lancelot passes by her castle she looks directly at him and brings about her fate. Desiring to meet him, she leaves her tower and rides a boat to his home of Camelot. She dies before reaching the shore. Here Waterhouse paints in the style and bright colours of the Pre-Raphaelite Brotherhood, though the group had disbanded several decades earlier.

Luke Fildes
The Doctor exhibited 1891

Fildes believed in the power of visual images to influence public opinion on subjects such as poverty and injustice, and his paintings of the hardships of working-class life were widely reproduced. In 1890 Henry Tate commissioned a painting from Fildes, and the artist chose a subject inspired by the death of his own son and the professional devotion shown by the doctor who treated him. Fildes invented a new setting for his painting, and to make the picture convincing he constructed a cottage interior in his studio, beginning work at dawn each day to catch the light effect he wanted.

Walter Richard Sickert
Minnie Cunningham at the Old Bedford 1892

Sickert painted the ordinary life he saw around him. He was influenced by impressionist artists such as Edgar Degas, whom he had met in Paris. Minnie Cunningham was a popular performer at the Old Bedford Music Hall in Camden Town, London. Sickert went there regularly and made dozens of sketches capturing the effects of light and movement on the stage and in the auditorium.

Gwen John
Self-Portrait 1902

John trained at the Slade School of Art in London, and this work was painted soon after she left. In a profession still largely dominated by men John was exceptional in establishing a successful artistic career, although overshadowed at the time by her brother Augustus. John grew up in Wales but lived in France for most of her life. She was part of the artistic community in Paris – the European centre of new developments in art – but preferred to work in solitude.

Duncan Grant
Bathing 1911

Duncan Grant was a member of the 'Bloomsbury Group' of artists. He painted this work as part of a decorative scheme for the dining room at the Borough Polytechnic in London. The theme was 'London on Holiday', and Grant responded with this idealised panorama of seven male bathing nudes. The nudes represented the continuous movement of a single figure. Grant's design was inspired by the Italian classical sculptor Michelangelo's male nudes and summers spent at the Serpentine in Hyde Park, which was a site associated with London's gay culture. *Bathing* was seen as controversial at the time, because of its homoerotic implications.

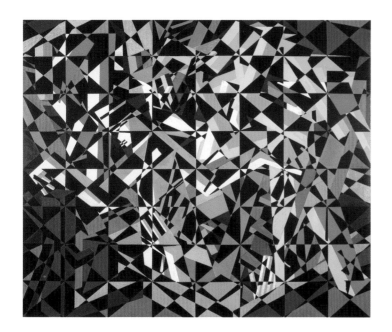

David Bomberg
In the Hold c.1913–14

The son of Polish Jewish immigrants, Bomberg grew up in East London. In this work he demonstrates his search for a way to use a language of pure form to express the modern urban environment. The work is based on a scene of dockers working in the hold of a ship. In the centre left can be seen one of the dockworkers, wearing a hat. Bomberg has used a geometrical framework to turn the subject of the picture into dynamic angles.

Mark Gertler
Merry-Go-Round 1916

Uniformed men and women in rigid poses, their mouths crying in silent unison, are trapped on a carousel that revolves endlessly. This work was painted at the height of the First World War, and here Gertler has taken the conflict as his subject. Gertler – a conscientious objector – lived near London's Hampstead Heath and was inspired by an annual fair held there for wounded soldiers. He said, 'Lately the whole horror of war has come freshly upon me.' The fairground ride, traditionally associated with pleasure and entertainment, is horrifically transformed into a metaphor for the relentless military machine.

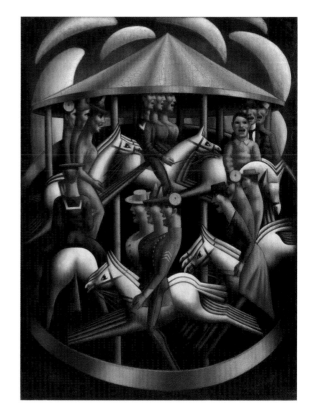

Stanley Spencer
The Resurrection, Cookham 1924–7

The setting here is the village churchyard in Cookham, Berkshire, where Spencer was born and spent much of his life. Christ sits in the church porch, cradling three babies. God stands behind him, while all around the dead are resurrected. Spencer himself appears near the centre, naked, leaning against a grave stone, and his partner Hilda lies sleeping in a bed of ivy. At the top left, risen souls are transported to Heaven in boats along the River Thames. Spencer referred to Cookham as 'a village in Heaven' in which everything was invested with mystical significance.

Ben Nicholson
1935 (white relief) 1935

Nicholson was interested in the ways in which painting can represent space. This is one of a number of shallow relief works he made in the 1930s in which light and shadow play between areas of different depth. Colour is reduced to white, a symbol of purity and the colour of modernity. Nicholson was a leading figure in the international modernist movement, whose concerns related to new ideas about living, and especially to modern architecture, in which natural light and simplicity of form were major concerns.

Ronald Moody
Johanaan 1936

Moody came to Britain from Jamaica in 1923 to train as a dentist. He was profoundly inspired by the British Museum's ethnographic collections, in particular the 'tremendous inner force, the irresistible movement in stillness' of Egyptian sculpture. Not having the financial means for formal training, he taught himself first to model in clay and then, in the early 1930s, to carve. He held successful exhibitions in Paris, moving there in 1938; he left in 1940 after the outbreak of the Second World War and returned to Britain. This work was made in Paris and took a year to carve from a single block of elm.

HENRY MOORE

Henry Moore emerged in the 1920s as a radical and experimental figure and rapidly became established as the leading British sculptor of his generation. His enduring subject was the human body, through which he believed 'one can express more completely one's feelings about the world than in any other way'. Moore's work was also associated with landscape and nature: he saw the countryside as the best setting for his sculptures, and his forms often derive their shape from natural objects such as stones, bones and sticks.

Mask 1929 (left)

This work points to Moore's interest in the sculpture he saw on his regular visits to the ethnographic collections at the British Museum. He cast it in concrete, a relatively new sculptural material that had previously been primarily used as a building material.

Recumbent Figure 1938 (bottom left)

This is one of the earliest works in which Moore shows the female figure undulating like a landscape. It was commissioned to stand in the grounds of a house near the Sussex Downs. Visually, the figure would have acted as a bridge between the rolling hills and the modern architecture of the house. Moore often worked with British stone, and this Hornton stone came from a quarry near Banbury in Oxfordshire.

King and Queen 1952–3, cast 1957 (top right)

Moore suggested that the idea for this work came from ancient Egyptian statues and from fairy tales he read to his daughter. It was made about the same time as the coronation of Queen Elizabeth II, but it seems to focus more on the ancient conception of the monarch as a divine being.

Shelterers in the Tube 1941 (right)

Moore's wartime drawings of Londoners sheltering underground secured his public reputation and became famous symbols of the Blitz and of British stoicism in adversity.

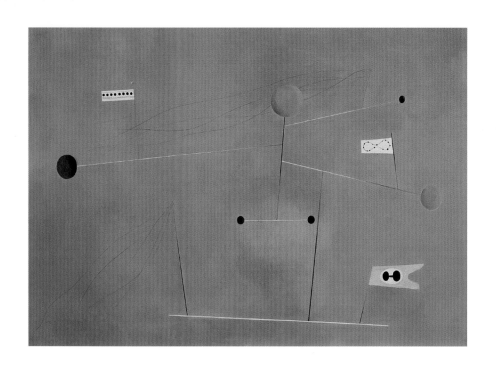

Paule Vézelay
Construction. Grey Lines on Pink Ground 1938

Paule Vézelay was born Marjorie Watson-Williams, adopting her new name in 1926 when she moved to Paris. She became part of an international network of leading experimental artists in France. Though she did not find the same success when she returned to Britain, she is now seen as one of the pioneers of British abstract art. This work encompasses what Vézelay saw as the most basic artistic language: curved and straight lines. It shows how the simplest of forms can suggest both space and movement.

Naum Gabo
Construction in Space with Crystalline Centre 1938–40

Gabo was one of the first sculptors to construct works rather than carving or modelling them. He also pioneered the use of plastic as an art medium. He was friends with a chemist working in the plastics industry and so enjoyed privileged access to some of the latest materials of the time. This work, made from transparent sheets of Perspex wrapped around thinner sheets of celluloid, answers his desire to 'express the dynamic interior of objects'. Russian-born Gabo lived in London from 1936, relocating to Cornwall with the outbreak of the Second World War.

Jacob Epstein
Jacob and the Angel 1940–1

Epstein was an important figure in the development of 20th-century sculpture, challenging traditional subjects and taking inspiration from west Africa and Asia. The subject here comes from a story in Genesis which tells how Jacob was forced to wrestle through the night with an unknown assailant. In the morning his opponent revealed himself to be an angel and messenger from God. Here, the angel is supporting Jacob, who has just collapsed. The subject of Jacob wrestling with the angel fascinated Epstein and may have had some personal significance for him, not least because he shared a name with the character.

BARBARA HEPWORTH

Barbara Hepworth was one of the leading sculptors of the 20th century, gaining prominence in the 1920s as a modern abstract artist. In the 1930s she moved to St Ives in Cornwall with her husband, the artist Ben Nicholson. Her work has come to be associated principally with the art of St Ives and her experience of the sea and landscape of that place. In the 1950s and 1960s she continued to exhibit widely, winning major international awards and commissions.

Forms in Echelon 1938 (left)

This work relates to Hepworth's interest in situating sculpture in the landscape: an early photograph of the piece shows it superimposed onto a photograph of a garden. 'The sculpture has an upward growth but the curves of the two monoliths make a closed composition which, in the open, with light all round … create a quietness, a pause in the progress of the eye,' Hepworth said.

Pelagos 1946 (right)

Pelagos (meaning 'sea' in Greek) was inspired by a view of the bay at St Ives, where two arms of land enfold the sea on either side. The hollowed-out wood has a spiral formation resembling a shell, a wave or the roll of a hill. Hepworth wanted the taut strings to express 'the tension I felt between myself and the sea, the wind or the hills'.

Sea Form (Porthmeor) 1958 (below)

Porthmeor is a beach close to Hepworth's studio in St Ives. It has been said that this sculpture 'seems to belong to the living world of the sea'. The curling top lip of the bronze is like a breaking wave, while the green and white patina of the inner surface recalls the colours of the sea and surf.

Graham Sutherland
Green Tree Form: Interior of Woods 1940

Sutherland is best known for his organic
landscapes of the Pembrokeshire coast.
This work is based on a tree fallen
across a grassy bank, its roots exposed.
Sutherland isolated this 'found object'
and abstracted its shape so that it
seems to loom from the murky green
surroundings. It resembles a monster
or even a truncated human figure.
Writing about his process, Sutherland
said, 'The prototype in nature has got
to be seen through the terms of art.
A metamorphosis has got to take place.'

L.S. Lowry
The Pond 1950

Lowry worked as a rent collector and painted the urban landscapes of Salford and Manchester which he knew well. This work contains many features typical of Lowry's work: smoking chimneys, terraced houses and figures swarming through the city's streets and open spaces. Though he is often seen as a realist, his works were largely composed from a variety of repeated elements. The artist said of this work, 'I hadn't the slightest idea of what I was going to put in the canvas when I started the picture but it eventually came out as you see it. This is the way I like working best.'

FRANCIS BACON

Francis Bacon, who was born in Dublin, is best
known for the emotionally charged, raw imagery
of his paintings. His figures are typically isolated
in geometric, cage-like spaces, set against flat,
nondescript backgrounds. Bacon said that he saw
images 'in series', and his work typically focused
on a single subject for sustained periods.

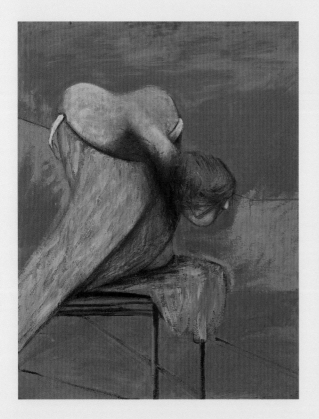

Three Studies for Figures at the Base of a Crucifixion c.1944 (left and below)

The title of this triptych refers to figures sometimes depicted at the foot of the cross in paintings of Christ's Crucifixion. Bacon later related them to the Eumenides, the vengeful Furies of Greek myth. The first exhibition of this work, in April 1945, coincided with the public release of the first photographs and film footage of the Nazi concentration camps. For some, this work reflected the pessimistic world ushered in by the Holocaust and the advent of nuclear weapons.

Study for a Portrait 1952 (above)

Bacon often based his paintings on photographic images. One source for the figure in this work is a film still from the Soviet director Sergei Eisenstein's *Battleship Potemkin* (1925) showing a screaming woman in smashed glasses. Bacon was fascinated by the expressive power of the mouth.

Lucian Freud
Girl with a White Dog 1950–1

Freud was born in Berlin, the grandson
of the psychoanalyst Sigmund Freud.
This early portrait shows the artist's
first wife, Kitty Garman, when she was
pregnant. A close relationship with
his sitters was important for Freud,
and they often sat for him for many
hours. He said his early work emerged
from his 'visual aggression' with sitters,
claiming, 'I would sit very close and
stare. It could be uncomfortable for
both of us.' The absence of a name in
the title emphasises the analytic quality
of the artist's observation, despite his
intimate connection to the subject.

Prunella Clough
Man Hosing Metal Fish Boxes 1951

Clough was fascinated by the urban and industrial landscape. Her paintings captured the working lives of labourers and scrutinised the surfaces and textures of the contemporary environment. She found her subjects by touring industrial wastelands and bombsites – docks, power stations, factories and scrapyards. The subject of this work is thought to stem from her visits to the coast of East Anglia but, although inspired by a certain locality, Clough's work turns the particular and localised into something more universal.

F.N. Souza
Crucifixion 1959

Souza was born into a Catholic family in the Portuguese colony of Goa in western India. In the 1950s he was among the first of the post-Independence generation of Indian artists to establish a career in Britain. Souza's depiction of Christ as a skeletal and menacing figure addresses his own feelings of religious conflict and rejects the sanitised European-looking Christ figures conventionally depicted in Western religious painting.

Peter Blake
Self-Portrait with Badges 1961

At the core of Blake's work is a fascination with the world of popular culture and entertainment, including music, film and sport. This self-portrait shows his interest in America with objects such as the denim jacket (rare in Britain at the time), baseball boots, badges and the magazine dedicated to Elvis Presley, who had just become well known in Britain. Blake uses these items rather like a 17th-century portrait painter, to suggest his interests or achievements.

Peter Lanyon
Wreck 1963

Lanyon was a Cornish painter who developed a method of abstract painting based on the landscape and his experience of particular places. The inspiration for this painting came from the 1962 wreck of a French trawler, *Jeanne Gougy*, which ran aground at Land's End in stormy weather. It was one of the most dramatic wreck and rescue events to have taken place along the Cornish coast, and Lanyon took his family to see the wreck a few days after it occurred. The layered and gestural surface of the painting invokes the turbulent sea and the complex interplay of natural forces.

Anthony Caro
The Window 1966–7

Caro pioneered the creation of abstract sculpture made from industrial materials. He removed the sculpture from its plinth and placed it directly on the floor, with the aim of removing the barrier between the work and the viewer, who is invited to approach and interact with the sculpture from all sides. In this work, large rectangular sheets of steel made from solid and mesh steel are arranged with horizontal and vertical beams to form an enclosure with an opening at one corner. The viewer is invited into the space, but, Caro said, 'by the eyes only'. It is our imagination that Caro invites through the window, not our feet.

Frank Bowling
Mirror 1966

Guyana-born Bowling studied at the Royal College of Art (1959–62) and the staircase in this painting was one in the art school when it was housed above the Victoria and Albert Museum. The work combines a figurative approach with a more abstract dimension. Bowling painted it at a key moment in his career, as he was moving away from figurative work and developing an increasingly abstract style. *Mirror* stages the artist's engagement with these different approaches to painting. Two of the three descending figures are self-portraits, and the one in the middle represents Paddy Kitchen, Bowling's wife at the time.

Bridget Riley
Deny II 1967

Riley began to develop her signature op art style in the early 1960s, exploring how we see shapes and patterns and the disorienting effect on the eye they can produce. In this work she explores the effects produced by the contrast of different 'warm' and 'cold' greys. The background is a uniform dark grey upon which a grid of small ovals rotates and changes tone. A 'V' shape appears; and though it is only the ovals that are getting darker, and not the background, too, our eyes seem to deny this.

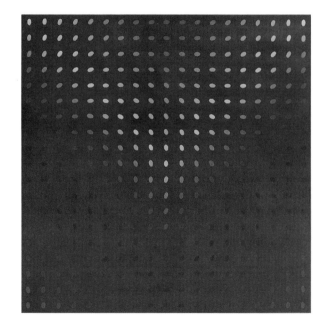

Richard Long
A Line Made by Walking 1967

Long often makes work in response to his experience of the landscape and ideas of impermanence, time, distance and measurement. Here, he walked backwards and forwards between two points in a Wiltshire field until the flattened grass became visible as a line. He photographed the line, recording his physical intervention in the landscape.

A LINE MADE BY WALKING

ENGLAND 1967

Richard Hamilton
Swingeing London 67 (f) 1968–9

Hamilton is widely regarded as a founder of pop art. He incorporated images from film posters, magazines and art history in his art and was interested in architecture and design, as well as broader political subjects. This work is based on a photograph, taken from a newspaper, showing Mick Jagger handcuffed to the art dealer Robert Fraser following their appearance in court on drugs charges. Both were convicted. The title plays on the term 'Swinging London' and the judge's insistence on imposing a swingeing penalty. For many, this occasion typified the moral backlash against the liberalisation of the 1960s.

DAVID HOCKNEY

David Hockney is one of the most popular and widely recognised artists of our time. Originally from Bradford in Yorkshire, he was a student in London from 1959 to 1962 and moved to Los Angeles later in the 1960s, splitting his time between Britain and California. Hockney's main interest is the challenge of representation: how do we see the world, and how can that world of time and space be captured in two dimensions?

A Bigger Splash 1967 (below)

The 1960s are often seen as a time when Britain emerged from the greyness of the post-war years into a period of optimism, youthfulness and colour. Few works exemplify this perception better than Hockney's depictions of Californian swimming pools. They evoke a glamorous and exotic life of sun and leisure. Frequently, Hockney populates these scenes with male figures, but here only the splash suggests a human presence. The painting also reflects Hockney's concern with capturing in paint transparent materials and transient moments.

Mr and Mrs Clark and Percy 1970–1
(above)

The textile designer Celia Birtwell and fashion designer Ossie Clark were close friends with Hockney, who was best man at their wedding in 1969. Here he paints them in their flat, surrounded by personal objects. In a reversal of traditional wedding portraits, Birtwell is shown standing while Clark is seated, perhaps hinting at the unconventional nature of their (short-lived) marriage.

My Parents 1977
(right)

Painted a year before the death of Hockney's father, this work is a subtle exploration of human behaviour and family relationships. While Hockney's mother poses readily for her son, his father, who fidgeted during sittings, is shown reading. A postcard of the Renaissance painter Piero della Francesca's *Baptism of Christ* is reflected in the mirror. In an earlier version Hockney included a self-portrait in this mirror, inserting himself between the figures of his parents.

Gilbert & George
Red Morning Trouble 1977

The individual views here of Gilbert & George show them contemplating and looking inwards. They depict themselves inside a grid made up of images of blossoming trees and the cityscape of London. When the colour red appears in the otherwise black-and-white photographs of Gilbert & George's work of this time it signals an emotional and political response to their subject. The addition of the word 'Trouble' to the title (other works in the group have titles such as *Red Morning Hell* or *Red Morning Hate*), injects a feeling of violence, misery and dread into images that might otherwise seem serene or commonplace.

Jo Spence (in collaboration with Terry Dennett)
The Highest Product of Capitalism (after John Heartfield) 1979

This photograph shows Spence standing in front of a shop window holding a sign that reads 'I'll Take (Almost) Any Work'. It was inspired by *The Finest Product of Capitalism* 1932 by the artist John Heartfield. In Heartfield's work a man wearing a sign declaring 'Any work accepted' stands in front of an image of a woman wearing an opulent wedding dress. Spence has exchanged the man for herself – which makes us think about women's position in the workplace and more specifically her own work as a commercial photographer, ten years earlier.

Antony Gormley
Untitled (for Francis) 1985

The body has been the major subject of Antony Gormley's art. He uses his own body to examine the physical and spiritual relationships between humankind and the natural world. This sculpture is a plaster mould of the artist's body, reinforced with fibreglass and encased in a skin of soldered lead. The pose here resembles that of a Christian saint receiving the stigmata (the wounds of Christ) but rather than in the side, as tradition dictates, the wound is in the breast. Gormley says, 'sculpture, for me, uses the physical as a means to talk about the spirit … a visual means to refer to things which cannot be seen'.

Lubaina Himid
The Carrot Piece 1985

Himid, winner of the 2017 Turner Prize, makes works which, as she puts it, acknowledge 'the contribution black people have made to cultural life in Europe for the past several hundred years'. Here, a white man fails to tempt a black woman with a carrot. Her arms are already full with everything she needs. Himid says the provisions the woman carries are 'inherited wisdom, education and love'. She says the work 'refers to the choices available when trying to force people to do things they have no desire to do – the carrot or the stick: the man on the unstable unicycle has both; the woman will be persuaded by neither.'

Black Audio Film Collective
Handsworth Songs 1986

This film is a richly layered documentary representing the hopes and dreams of post-war black British people in the light of the civil disturbances of the 1980s. It engages with Britain's colonial past, public and private memories, and the struggles of race and class. The title refers to the riots in Handsworth, Birmingham during September 1985 and the institutional response to them. The soundtrack is influenced by reggae, punk and the post-industrial noise movement. Black Audio Film Collective was founded in 1982 by a group of sociology, psychology and fine art students. The collective undertook all aspects of the production and distribution of their films.

Damien Hirst
The Acquired Inability to Escape 1991

Hirst's work deals with dilemmas of human existence, including the fragility of life and society's reluctance to confront death. An office table and chair are enclosed in a steel-framed glass vitrine, or cell. On the table are a packet of cigarettes, a lighter and an ashtray. According to Hirst, cigarettes relate to the cyclical nature of life, the cigarette representing life and the ashtray death. The inevitability of death is also evoked by the entrapment suggested by the title, and confirmed by the enclosed glass cell.

'Everything is connected in life...' from the series *Signs that Say What You Want Them To Say and Not Signs that Say What Someone Else Wants You To Say* 1992–3

Wearing's photographs explore how the public and private identities of ordinary people are self-fashioned and documented. This work is one of a series in which Wearing stood on a busy street and asked passers-by to write down what was on their mind. She then photographed them holding their statements. A broad cross-section of people participated in the photographs. The series provides a fascinating social and historical document as it refers to the economic decline in Britain in the early 1990s as well as the expression of intimate thoughts or personal convictions.

Sarah Lucas
Pauline Bunny 1997

Lucas's work challenges everyday gender stereotyping and sexism, often through the language and media of popular culture. She uses visual puns and humour, often in sculptures made from an unexpected range of commonplace materials, such as worn furniture, clothing, cigarettes, fruit and vegetables. This work was originally exhibited as part of a larger piece consisting of eight similar 'bunny girl' figures limply arranged around a snooker table. To be 'snookered', in the language of the game, means to be prevented from 'scoring'. The limp, floppy form undermines the fantasy of the glamorous 'bunny girl'.

Chris Ofili
No Woman, No Cry 1998

This work is a tribute to the London teenager Stephen Lawrence, who was murdered in a racially motivated attack in 1993. A public inquiry into the murder investigation concluded that the Metropolitan Police force was institutionally racist. In each of the tears shed by the woman in the painting is a collaged image of Lawrence's face, while the words 'RIP Stephen Lawrence' are just discernible beneath the layers of paint. As well as this specific reference, the artist intended the painting to be read as a universal portrayal of melancholy and grief.

Peter Doig
Echo Lake 1998

Doig's landscapes are often inspired by movie scenes, newspaper clippings, photographs and record covers. This work, like many of his paintings from this time, is based on horizontal bands of colour overlaid with detail. A policeman stands on the shoreline and shouts across a lake in the direction of the viewer. The title suggests that nothing comes back to him but his own voice. The mirrored reflection on the water provides a visual version of the echo. Doig has said that 'reflections function as entrances to other worlds'. This work stages distress and unease in a contemporary setting.

Rachel Whiteread
Untitled (Stairs) 2001

Whiteread casts the space inside or around everyday forms. This work is a very large free-standing sculpture made up of ten elements bolted together. It is the cast of the staircase in her home and the space above it, including three square-shaped landings as the stairs zigzag down the stairwell. It has been rotated by 90 degrees so that it stands on what would have been a wall in the original space. Whiteread was drawn to the stairs of the building, a former synagogue in East London, as a space which bears witness to the comings and goings of daily life.

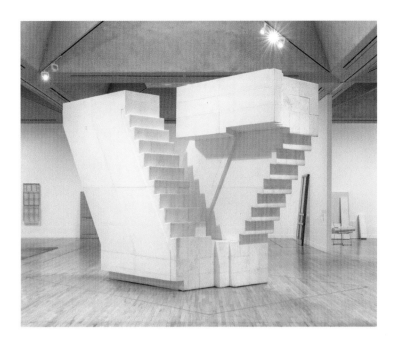

Rebecca Warren
Come, Helga 2006

Warren's unfired clay forms question the sculptural traditions that surround the use of particular materials. They also challenge accepted norms of the ideal figure. Her work is both playful and expressive: gouged and kneaded, lumpy and messy. This work shows two female figures standing side by side. Making reference to a range of sources, from Edgar Degas's ballerinas to fashion photographers and cartoonists, the exaggerated proportions of their bodies invoke clichés of the sexualised representation of women. However, the confrontational pose of the women is aggressive and confident, complicating the way in which the work can be understood.

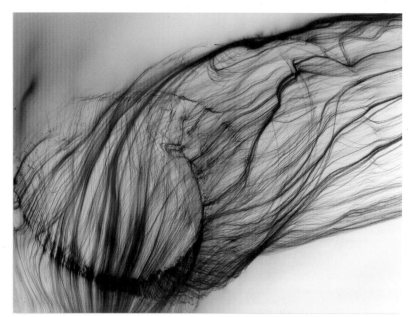

Wolfgang Tillmans
Freischwimmer 16 2003

The title of this photograph by German artist Wolfgang Tillmans literally refers to what was once an early stage of German swimming proficiency tests, but it also means something close to the English expression 'standing on your own two feet'. Tillmans created it in the darkroom without a camera or negative by tracing light directly onto photographic paper. He encourages us to think about what a photograph is – shouldn't it reproduce what we can see? Tillmans has enlarged the photograph to almost 2.5 metres long, making it the size of 19th-century history paintings. Classically, the large format reveals the detail in the composition, but here there is nothing more, and we are left to find meaning for ourselves.

Steve McQueen
Static 2009

McQueen is a BAFTA and Academy Award winning film director, screenwriter and video artist. This work is a digital projection on a seven-minute loop. Shot from a helicopter ceaselessly circling around the Statue of Liberty in New York, the film alternates between close-up and distance shots that show the monument looming over docks and buildings. In contrast to the perpetual movement of the camera, the title suggests a fixed perspective and a lack of movement. Through its close and relentless scrutiny, *Static* calls into question the monument's ability to maintain its status as a symbol of freedom and liberty unscathed.

Lynette Yiadom-Boakye
The Generosity 2010

Yiadom-Boakye paints portraits of imaginary people and places, carefully constructed without the help of photographs, models or sketches. Connections may be hinted at, but she provides no explanation of what the underlining story might be. Here, the title encourages us to read a narrative into the painting and to speculate about the relationship between the two figures and their actions – has one just received socks from the other, or is he about to give his socks to him? She is interested in issues of representation, particularly in connection with the depiction of the black subject in the history of European painting.

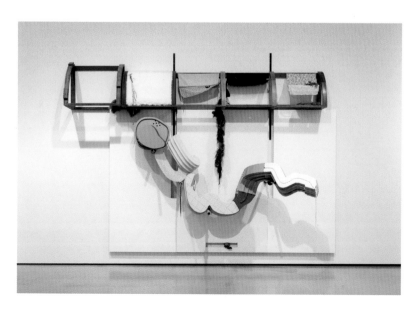

Helen Marten
Guild of Pharmacists 2014

Marten produces installations from handmade and found objects drawn from daily life. Her ideas arise from a broad range of references such as advertising, the internet and technology. Here carved and lacquered wood is arranged in a snake-like shape based on a traditional pharmacist's sign. Objects sit on the support, reinforcing the sense of display, which Marten describes as 'a shop-front panorama'.

TATE MODERN
TATE LIVERPOOL
TATE ST IVES

Tate Modern – with its pioneering collection, ground-breaking international exhibitions, innovative commissions and inspiring events – is the world's most visited museum of modern and contemporary art. Since opening in 2000 it has transformed attitudes to the visual arts, and its exciting expansion in 2016 and the opening of the Blavatnik building has reinforced its reputation as one of the UK's most important sites for visitors.

Tate Liverpool is dedicated to international modern and contemporary art. Opening in 1988, the building was converted from a former warehouse on the Albert Dock, once a key hub for international trade. With an active education programme, the gallery encourages a new, younger audience. Major exhibitions have included surveys of work by Jackson Pollock, Andy Warhol, Francis Bacon, Sarah Lucas, Gustav Klimt and Piet Mondrian.

Tate St Ives is located on the coast of Cornwall, in a town whose unique landscape and quality of light have attracted artists since Victorian times. Overlooking Porthmeor Beach and facing out to the Atlantic Ocean, the gallery celebrates the remarkable variety of artists who lived or worked in the area, including Alfred Wallis, Ben Nicholson, Naum Gabo and Barbara Hepworth, whose former studio is now a Museum and Sculpture Garden managed by Tate.

CREDITS

All works in copyright are © the artist/s unless otherwise stated.

Francis Bacon Presented by Eric Hall 1953 (N06171), © Tate, pp.44–5 (bottom); Bequeathed by Simon Sainsbury 2006, accessioned 2008 (T12616), © The Estate of Francis Bacon. All rights reserved, DACS 2018, p.45 (top)

Mary Beale Purchased 1992 (T06612), p.9

John Bettes Purchased 1897 (N01496), p.6

Black Audio Film Collective Presented by Tate Members 2008 (T12862), p.56

Peter Blake Presented by the Moores Family Charitable Foundation to celebrate the John Moores Liverpool Exhibition 1979 (T02406), © Peter Blake. All rights reserved, DACS 2018, p.48

William Blake Presented by Mrs John Richmond 1922 (A00035), p.14 (top); Bequeathed by W. Graham Robertson 1949 (N05889), p.14 (bottom); Presented by W. Graham Robertson 1939 (N05058), p.15 (top); Presented by Miss Mary H. Dodge through the Art Fund 1918 (N03340), p.15 (bottom)

David Bomberg Presented by the Friends of the Tate Gallery 1967 (T00913), © Tate, p.33

Frank Bowling Presented by the artist, Rachel Scott, and their 4 children Benjamin and Sacha Bowling, Marcia and Iona Scott 2013 (T13936), p.50

Martin Boyce Commissioned with the support of the Clore Duffield Foundation, p.3

Edward Coley Burne-Jones Bequeathed by Lord Battersea 1924 (N04005), p.25

Anthony Caro Accepted by H.M. Government in Lieu of Inheritance Tax from the collection of the late Sir Anthony Caro, offered from the estate of Lady Caro (Sheila Girling) and allocated to Tate 2017 (T14953), © Courtesy Barford Sculptures Ltd., p.49

Cholmondeley Ladies (Unknown Artist) Presented anonymously 1955 (T00069), p.7

Prunella Clough Accepted by H.M. Government in lieu of tax and allocated to the Tate Gallery 1993 (T06673), © Estate of Prunella Clough, p.47

John Constable Purchased by Tate with assistance from the National Lottery through the Heritage Lottery Fund, The Manton Foundation, Art Fund (with a contribution from the Wolfson Foundation) and Tate Members in partnership with Amgueddfa Cymru – National Museum Wales, Colchester and Ipswich Museums Service, National Galleries of Scotland, and the Salisbury Museum 2013 (T13896), p.21

John Singleton Copley Purchased 1864 (N00733), p.13

Richard Dadd Presented by Siegfried Sassoon in memory of his friend and fellow officer Julian Dadd, a great-nephew of the artist, and of his two brothers who gave their lives in the First World War 1963 (T00598), p.26

David Des Granges Purchased with assistance from the Friends of the Tate Gallery, the Art Fund and the Pilgrim Trust 1976 (T02020), p.7

Peter Doig Presented by the Trustees in honour of Sir Dennis and Lady Stevenson (later Lord and Lady Stevenson of Coddenham), to mark his period as Chairman 1989–98, 1998 (T07467), © Peter Doig. All rights reserved, DACS 2018, p.58

Anthony van Dyck Accepted by H.M. Government in lieu of tax with additional payment made with assistance from the Art Fund, the Patrons of British Art and Christopher Ondaatje 2002 (T07896), p.8

Jacob Epstein Purchased with assistance from the National Lottery through the Heritage Lottery Fund, the Art Fund and the Henry Moore Foundation 1996 (T07139), © Estate of Sir Jacob Epstein, p.39

Luke Fildes Presented by Sir Henry Tate 1894 (N01522), p.30

Lucian Freud Purchased 1952 (N06039), © Tate, p.46

Henry Fuseli Presented by Miss Julia Carrick Moore in accordance with the wishes of her sister 1887 (N01228), p.16

Naum Gabo Accepted by H.M. Government in lieu of tax and allocated to the Tate Gallery 1995 (T06977), © Nina & Graham Williams/Tate 2018, p.38

Thomas Gainsborough Purchased with assistance from the Friends of the Tate Gallery 1975 (T02000), p.12

Mark Gertler Purchased 1984 (T03846), p.33

Marcus Gheeraerts II Purchased with assistance from the Friends of the Tate Gallery, the Art Fund and the Pilgrim Trust 1980 (T03028), p.6

Gilbert & George Presented by Janet Wolfson de Botton 1996 to celebrate the Tate Gallery Centenary 1997 (T07155), p.54

Antony Gormley Purchased 1987 (T05004), p.55

Duncan Grant Purchased 1931 (N04567), © Tate, p.32

Richard Hamilton Purchased 1969 (T01144), © R. Hamilton. All rights reserved, DACS 2018 p.51

Barbara Hepworth Presented by the artist 1964 (T00698), p.40; Presented by the artist 1964 (T00699), p.41 (top); Presented by the artist 1967 (T00957), p.41 (bottom). All © Bowness

Lubaina Himid Purchased using funds provided by the 2014 Outset/Frieze Art Fair Fund to benefit the Tate Collection 2015 (T14192), p.55 and back cover

Damien Hirst Presented by the artist 2007 (T12748), © Damien Hirst and Science Ltd. All rights reserved, DACS 2018, p.56

David Hockney Purchased 1981 (T03254), p.52; Presented by the Friends of the Tate Gallery 1971 (T01269), p.53 (top); Purchased 1981 (T03255), p.53 (bottom)

William Hogarth Presented by the Duke of Westminster 1895 (N01464), p.10

William Holman Hunt Presented by Sir Colin and Lady Anderson through the Friends of the Tate Gallery 1976 (T02075), p.23

Gwen John Purchased 1942 (N05366), p.31

Angelica Kauffman Presented by Mrs M. Bernard 1967 (T00928), p.11

Peter Lanyon Presented by the Friends of the Tate Gallery 1983 (T03693), © Estate of Peter Lanyon. All rights reserved, DACS 2018, p.48

John Lavery Presented by Lord Duveen 1930 (N04553), p.4

Thomas Lawrence Presented by Mrs C. FitzHugh 1843 (N00188), p.17

Frederic Leighton Presented by the Trustees of the Chantrey Bequest 1877 (N01754), p.26

Peter Lely Purchased with assistance from the Art Fund 1955 (T00058), p.8

Richard Long Purchased 1976 (P07149), p.51

L.S. Lowry Presented by the Trustees of the Chantrey Bequest 1951 (N06032), © Estate of L.S. Lowry. All rights reserved, DACS 2018, p.43

Sarah Lucas Presented by the Patrons of New Art (Special Purchase Fund) through the Tate Gallery Foundation 1998 (T07437), p.57

Steve McQueen Purchased with assistance from Ivor Braka, Thomas Dane, Mrs Wendy Fisher and Zamyn 2011 (T13425), © Steve McQueen, courtesy the artist and Thomas Dane Gallery, London, p.60

Helen Marten Purchased with funds provided by Tate Members and Tate Patrons 2015 (T14455), © Helen Marten, courtesy Sadie Coles HQ, London, p.61

John Everett Millais Presented by Sir Henry Tate 1894 (N01506), p.22 and front cover (detail)

Ronald Moody Purchased 1992 (T06591), © Estate of Ronald Moody, p.35

Henry Moore Transferred from the Victoria & Albert Museum 1983 (T03762), p.36 (top); Presented by the Contemporary Art Society 1939 (N05387), p.36 (bottom); Presented by the Friends of the Tate Gallery with funds provided by Associated Rediffusion Ltd 1959 (T00228), p.37 (top); Presented by the War Artists Advisory Committee 1946 (N05712), p.37 (bottom). © The Henry Moore Foundation. All rights reserved, pp.36 (both), 37 (top)

Ben Nicholson Purchased with assistance from the Contemporary Art Society 1955 (T00049), © Angela Verren Taunt. All rights reserved, DACS 2018, p.34

Chris Ofili Purchased 1999 (T07502), © Chris Ofili, courtesy Victoria Miro Gallery, London, p.58

Joshua Reynolds Purchased (Building the Tate Collection fund) with assistance from the National Heritage Memorial Fund, Tate Members, the Art Fund (with a contribution from the Wolfson Foundation) and other donors 2005 (T12033), p.11

Bridget Riley Purchased 1976 (T02030), © Bridget Riley 2018. All rights reserved, courtesy Karsten Schubert, London, p.50

Dante Gabriel Rossetti Presented by Georgiana, Baroness Mount-Temple in memory of her husband, Francis, Baron Mount-Temple 1889 (N01279), p.25

John Singer Sargent Presented by the Trustees of the Chantrey Bequest 1887 (N01615), p.28

Jan Siberechts Purchased with assistance from the Art Fund and the Friends of the Tate Gallery 1995 (T06996), p.9

Walter Richard Sickert Purchased 1976 (T02039), p.30

John Simpson Presented by Robert Vernon 1847 (N00382), p.20

F.N. Souza Purchased 1993 (T06776), © Estate of F.N. Souza. All rights reserved, DACS 2018 p.47

Jo Spence Presented by Tate Patrons 2014 (P80406), © The Jo Spence Memorial Archive p.54

Stanley Spencer Presented by Lord Duveen 1927 (N04239), © Tate, p.34

Graham Sutherland Purchased 1940 (N05139), © Tate, p.42

Wolfgang Tillmans Presented by the artist 2005 (P20284), © Wolfgang Tillmans, courtesy Maureen Paley, London, p.60

J.M.W. Turner Accepted by the nation as part of the Turner Bequest 1856 (N00480), p.18; Accepted by the nation as part of the Turner Bequest 1856 (N00503), p.19 (top); Accepted by the nation as part of the Turner Bequest 1856 (N00530), p.19 (bottom)

Paule Vézelay Purchased 1973 (T01725), © Estate of Paule Vézelay p.38

Henry Wallis Bequeathed by Charles Gent Clement 1899 (N01685), p.24

Rebecca Warren Presented by Tate Patrons 2006 (T12258), © Rebecca Warren, courtesy Maureen Paley, London, p.59

John William Waterhouse Presented by Sir Henry Tate 1894 (N01543), p.29

Gillian Wearing Purchased 2000 (P78351), © Gillian Wearing, courtesy Maureen Paley, London, p.57

James Abbott McNeill Whistler Bequeathed by Miss Rachel and Miss Jean Alexander 1972 (T01571), p.27

Rachel Whiteread Purchased from funds provided by the Art Fund and Tate Members 2003 (T07939), p.59

Joseph Wright of Derby Bequeathed by Miss Agnes Ann Best 1925 (N04132), p.12

Lynette Yiadom-Boakye Presented by Tate Patrons 2012 (T13654), p.61

Photographic credits

All images are © Tate 2018, with the exception of the following: Courtesy Maureen Paley, London, p.59 (bottom); © Smoking Dogs Films, courtesy Lisson Gallery, p.56 (top); Tate Gallery Archive, p.5 (both); © Tate 2018. Photo: Lucy Dawkins, pp.8 (bottom), 30 (bottom), Mark Heathcote pp.14 (bottom), 18 (bottom), 24, 54 (top), Joe Humphrys pp.3, 9 (both), 14 (top), 15 (bottom), Roger Sinek p.62 (middle); Annik Wetter, courtesy Sadie Coles HQ, London, p.61 (bottom)

Please note that on occasion, because of temporary changes in display or exhibition loans, some works illustrated in this guide may not be available to view at Tate Britain.

Tate is a charity and relies on a large number of supporters – individuals, foundations, companies and public sector sources – to enable it to deliver its programme of activities, both on and off its gallery sites. This support is essential in order for Tate to acquire works of art for the collection, run education, outreach and exhibition programmes, care for the collection in storage and enable art to be displayed, both digitally and physically, inside and outside Tate. For more information, please visit: www.tate.org.uk/join-support

First published 2018 by order of the Tate Trustees by Tate Publishing, a division of Tate Enterprises Ltd, Millbank, London SW1P 4RG
www.tate.org.uk/publishing

A catalogue record for this book is available from the British Library

ISBN 978 1 84976 580 0

Written by Kirsteen McSwein, Curator, Interpretation, Tate Britain

Designed by Emma Garnsey

Colour reproduction by DL Imaging Ltd, London

Printed and bound by Cambrian Printers, Wales